LIGHTNING

SEYMOUR SIMON

Updated Edition

Smithsonian | Collins

An Imprint of HarperCollinsPublishers

To Chloe, Benjamin and Joel with love from Grandpa

PHOTO CREDITS

Permission to use the following photographs is gratefully acknowledged:
Pages 4, 7, 9, 17, 20, 21, Warren Faidley/Weatherstock; page 10, Johnny Autery; pages 11, 13, 25, 29, 31, Peter Menzel; pages 15, 19, Thomas Ives; page 23, Dan Osborne/University of Alaska at Fairbanks; page 27, F. K. Smith; page 32, R. Lewis/Weatherstock.
The name of the Smithsonian, Smithsonian Institution, and the sunburst logo
are registered trademarks of the Smithsonian Institution.
Collins is an imprint of HarperCollins Publishers.

Lightning
Copyright © 1997, 2006 by Seymour Simon
Manufactured in China. All rights reserved.

No part of this book may be used or reproduced in any manner whatsoever without written permission except in the case of brief
quotations embodied in critical articles and reviews. For information address HarperCollins Children's Books, a division of
HarperCollins Publishers, 195 Broadway, New York, NY 10007.
www.harperchildrens.com

Library of Congress Cataloging-in-Publication Data
Simon, Seymour.
Lightning / Seymour Simon.
p.   cm.
Summary: Photographs and text explore the natural phenomenon of lightning.
ISBN-10: 0-06-088438-X (trade bdg.) — ISBN-13: 978-0-06-088438-3 (trade bdg.)
ISBN-10: 0-06-088435-5 (pbk.) — ISBN-13: 978-0-06-088435-2 (pbk.)
1. Lightning—Juvenile literature. [1. Lightning.] 1.Title.
QC966.5.S56 1997   96-16962
551.319'2—dc20   CIP
                                                                                                    AC

14 15 16 SCP 20 19 18 17 16 15 14 13 12 11

❖

Revised Edition

Smithsonian Mission Statement

For more than 160 years, the Smithsonian has remained true to its mission, "the increase and diffusion of knowledge." Today the Smithsonian is not only the world's largest provider of museum experiences supported by authoritative scholarship in science, history, and the arts but also an international leader in scientific research and exploration. The Smithsonian offers the world a picture of America, and America a picture of the world.

Natural History Mission Statement

We inspire curiosity, discovery, and learning about nature and culture through outstanding research, collections, exhibitions, and education.

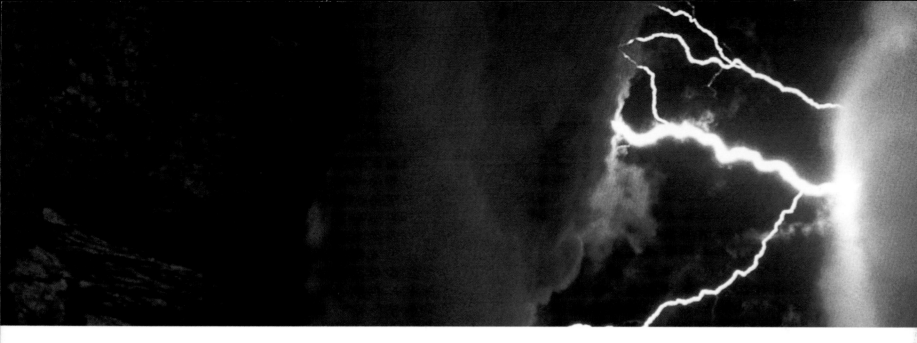

Every second of every day more than a hundred lightning bolts strike the earth. That's about ten million lightning bolts in a single day! The early Greeks thought that the king of the gods, Zeus, hurled thunderbolts from stormy skies. The Vikings imagined their god of weather, Thor, striking a powerful hammer against an anvil to produce thunder and lightning. Native American tribes believed that lightning was caused by the flashing feathers and flapping wings of the mighty Thunderbird. Today we know that lightning is a river of electricity rushing through an ocean of air. Yet scientists are still not sure of exactly what causes these awesome strokes of power.

Lightning bolts travel at "lightning" speeds of up to sixty thousand miles per second. That's six thousand times faster than our fastest spaceships. A single lightning bolt travels through twisted paths in the air about as wide as one of your fingers and from six to ten miles long.

A flash of lightning is brighter than ten million one-hundred-watt lightbulbs. And it pulses with hundreds of millions of volts and billions of watts, as much power as there is in all the electrical generating plants in the United States in that split second. But because the flash takes only a millionth of a second, the electricity in a bolt would power one lightbulb for only a month.

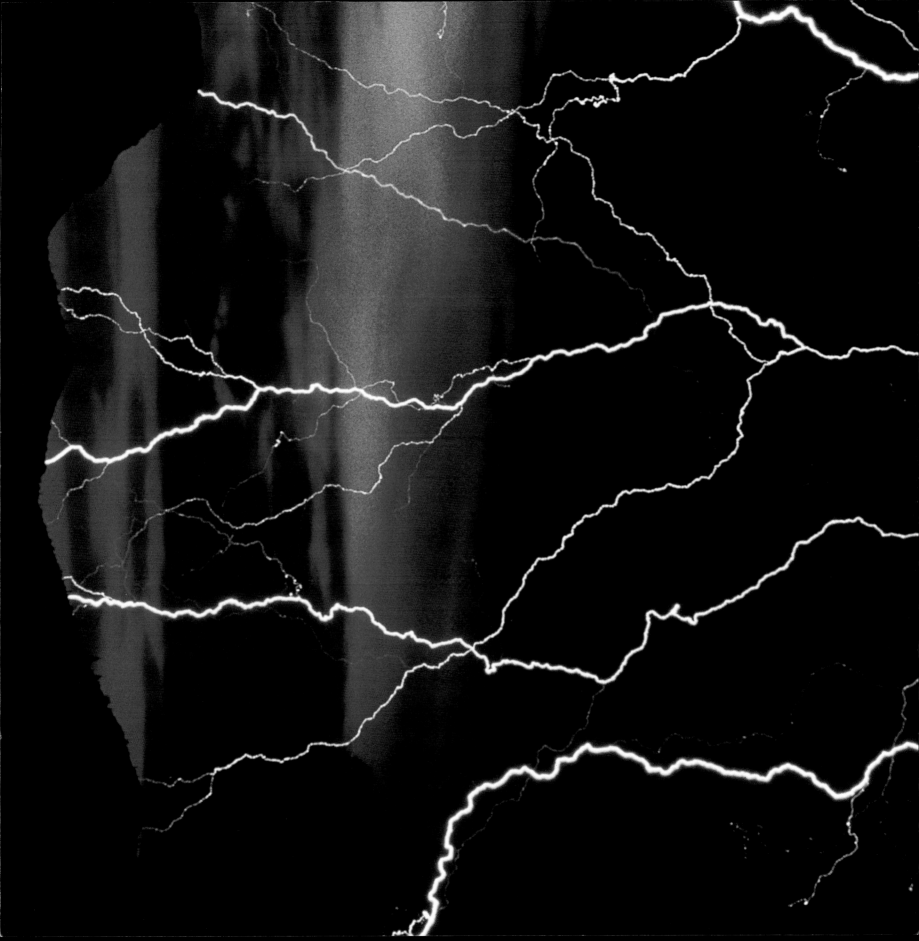

Lightning begins with violently moving ice crystals and raindrops in storm clouds. As a result of the motion, electric charges build up at the bottom of a cloud. An opposite electric charge builds up in the ground just below the cloud. The charges in the ground can make your hair stand on end right before a lightning storm.

Starting in the cloud, small streamers of sparks called *stepped leaders* begin to shoot downward in fifty-yard leaps. As the leaders approach the ground, they meet upward streamers from the ground, most likely from high places such as treetops and tall buildings. When the two streamers meet, their paths form a channel, and a lightning bolt is born. Though this kind of lightning seems to shoot down from the clouds, what we actually see is the return stroke of electricity flashing upward from the ground.

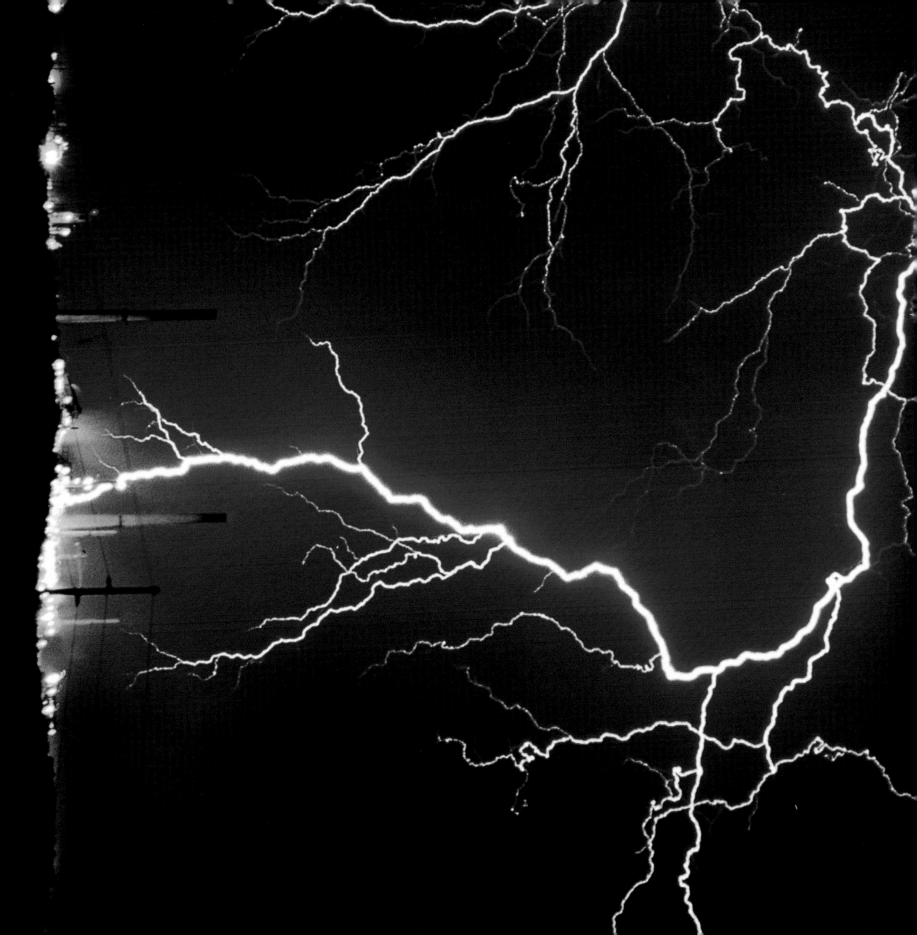

This fulgurite
was dug out
of the sand
in Arizona.

This is a photo of a lightning bolt striking a sixty-five-foot tree. Besides the main bolt, you can see two smaller upward discharges: one to the left of the main bolt, reaching up from the top branches, and another reaching up from the antenna on the farmhouse at the left. Trees sometimes survive direct hits because the electricity passes over their wet surface into the ground. Ten years after this tree was hit, it was still standing.

Lightning sometimes strikes the ground and tunnels downward into the soil. The intense heat of the electricity fuses the sand particles together into the shape of the bolt's path. The resulting tubular crust is called a *fulgurite*, after the Latin word for lightning. Some fulgurites are longer than ten feet.

Perhaps the most famous experiment to show that lightning is electrical took place in 1752, when Benjamin Franklin flew a kite during a Pennsylvania thunderstorm. As lightning flashed, sparks jumped from a key fastened to the bottom of the damp kite string. A silk ribbon attached to the string insulated Franklin's hand. The museum model seen in the photo demonstrates lightning striking a kite, which conducts the electricity to a bulb.

This highly dangerous experiment can be shown in a much safer way at home. On a dry day, drag your shoes along a carpet, then touch a metal doorknob and watch the spark jump! For an instant, you become a thundercloud by gathering charged particles called *electrons* from the carpet. When you reach for the doorknob, electrons stream from your hand in a tiny lightning bolt.

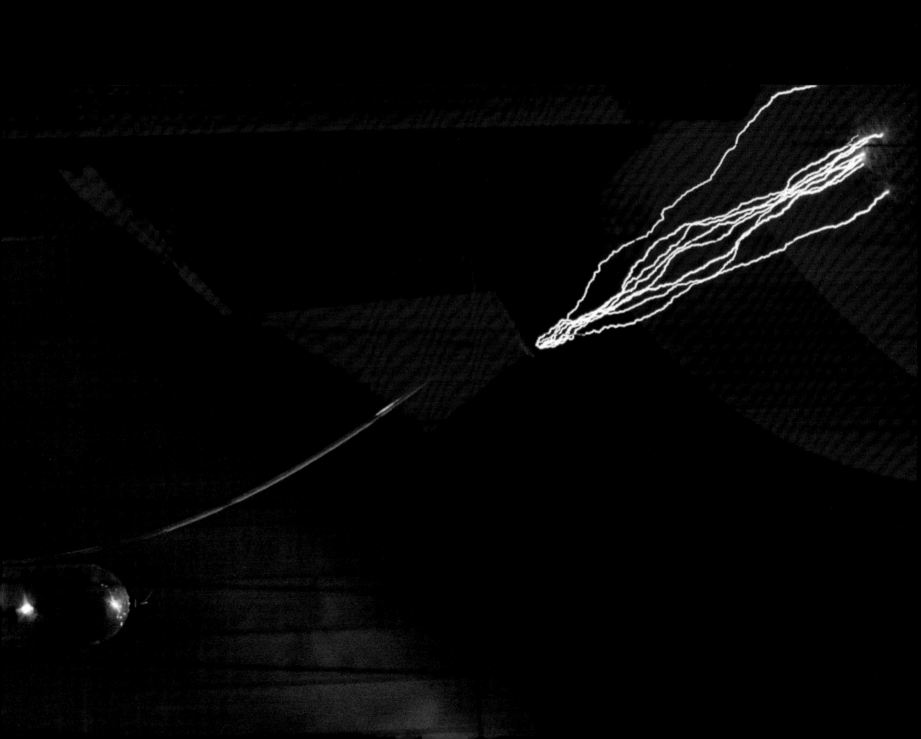

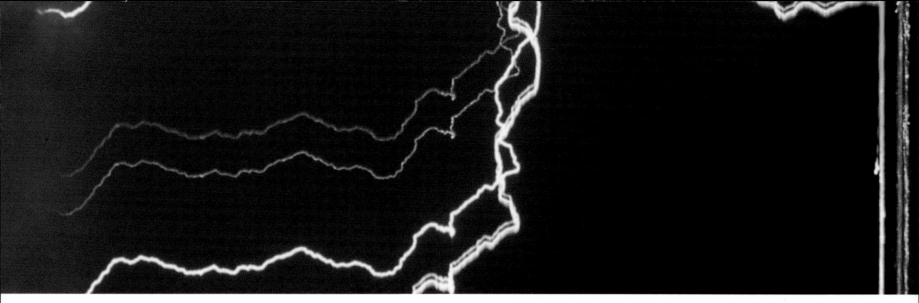

Scientists have replaced Franklin's kite and key with small rockets trailing long copper wires connected to electronic instruments. The rockets are launched from the ground into a passing storm cloud. The wire creates a path for the lightning bolt, and in an instant the wire is vaporized. The strike is measured and recorded by the instruments and safely studied by the scientists.

Photography is another useful tool scientists use to study lightning. A single lightning discharge is made up of twenty or more strokes, one after another in a fraction of a second. Swinging a camera with its shutter open during a lightning flash shows the many repeat strokes during a single flash. Each stroke takes place too fast for the eye to see, yet slow enough to make lightning seem to flicker.

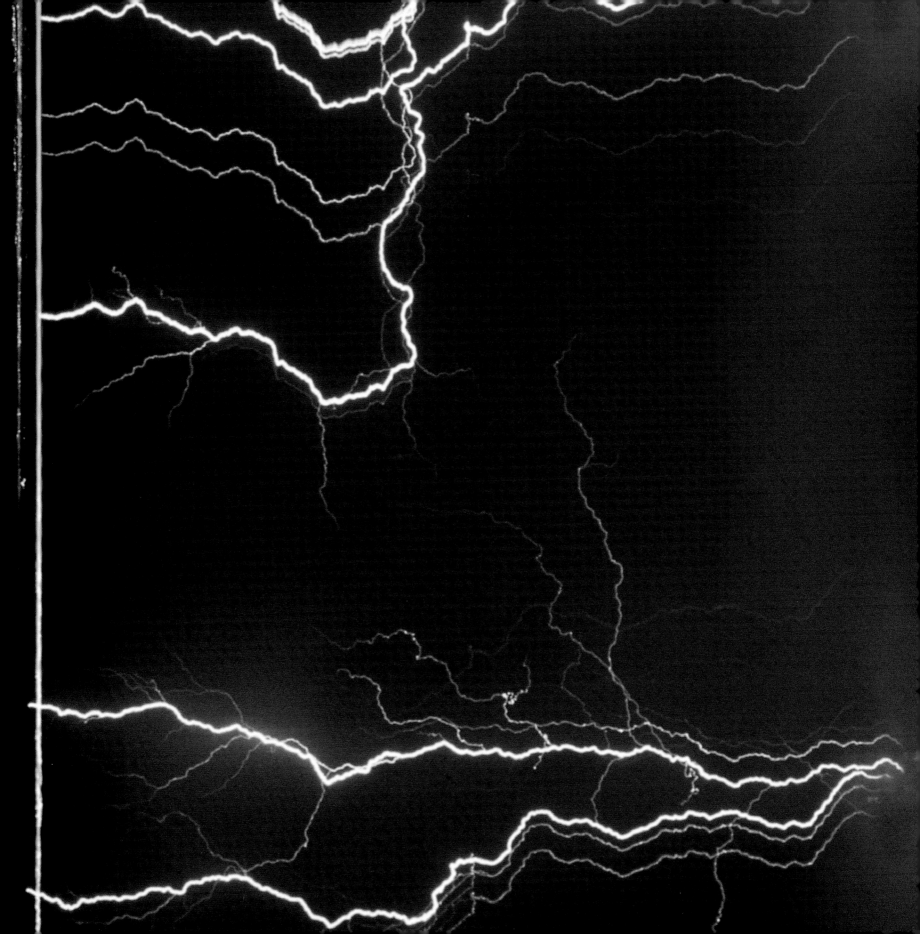

When a lightning bolt strikes, the electrical energy quickly changes into heat. Temperatures in the path of a lightning bolt can reach as high as fifty thousand degrees Fahrenheit, five times hotter than the surface of the sun.

The intense heat alongside the lightning channel makes the air expand explosively and then contract as it cools. The quick back and forth movement of air particles produces the sound waves we call thunder. From close up, we hear thunder as a single sharp crack. From farther away, thunder seems to roll or rumble in the distance.

When a lightning bolt flashes, we see it immediately, but thunder takes about five seconds to travel a mile. That's because light is about a million times faster than sound. Here's a way to measure how many miles lightning is from you. Start counting seconds when you see a lightning flash and stop when you hear the thunder. Just divide the number of seconds by five. So if you hear thunder five seconds after the flash, the lightning was one mile away; fifteen seconds means it was three miles away.

T here are three main kinds of lightning. *Intracloud lightning* is the most common. It occurs when lightning arcs between oppositely charged centers within the same cloud. From the outside, it looks as if the cloud suddenly flickers and brightens, then produces rumbling thunder. *Cloud-to-ground lightning* is the most dangerous form. It is the kind we know most about. The third kind, *intercloud lightning*, occurs when lightning leaps across a gap of clear air between two different clouds.

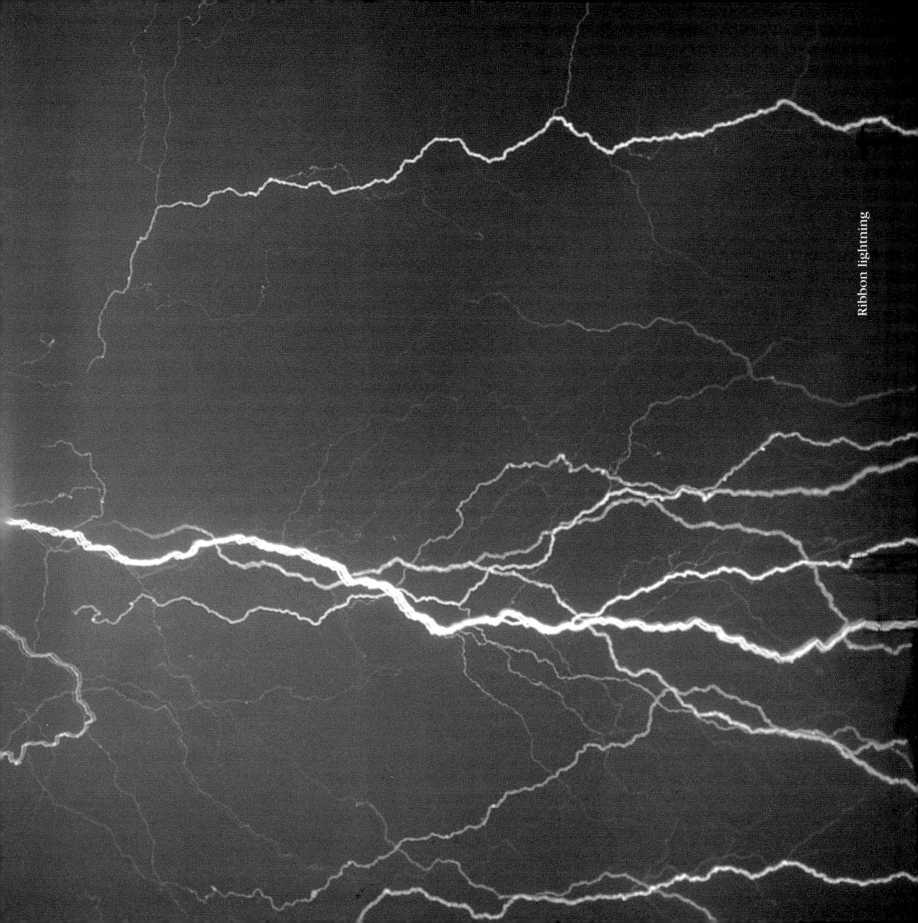

Ribbon lightning

Heat lightning

Ball lightning

You may have heard of other types of lightning. Usually these are just different names that describe when lightning comes or how it looks. For example, *heat lightning* occurs when it's hot, and *summer lightning* happens in the summer. *Sheet lightning* seems to come in flat waves, and *ribbon lightning* looks like streamers flashing through the sky. *Silent lightning* appears without a sound because it is so far away, and *colored lightning* seems to flash red or blue. *Ball lightning* is a bright round spark that seems to float in the air.

In the summer of 1995, scientists discovered a new kind of lightning, which they named *elves*. Elves are very bright short flashes of lightning that blaze forth high above the clouds at the very edge of space. They last for less than a thousandth of a second, quicker than you can blink. The color of elves is not yet known but is thought to be green.

Two other recently discovered high-altitude kinds of lightning are called *jets* and *sprites*. Jets are fast-moving fountains or sprays of blue light that burst upward from the tops of storm clouds to an altitude about twenty miles above the clouds. Pilots have reported seeing columns of blue or green light above thunderheads for years, but they have only recently been videotaped.

This is one of the first true-color images of a red sprite, photographed at an altitude sixty miles over a thunderstorm in the Midwest in July 1994. The white-blue flash below the sprite is normal lightning at the tops of the clouds.

The National Lightning Detection Network is a web of at least one hundred thirty magnetic direction finders that covers the entire United States. The detectors are used to locate cloud-to-ground lightning flashes. Information in the form of a grid map shows lightning across the country.

Spectacular lightning is common in Tucson, Arizona. During the summer's rainy season, thunderstorms can generate more than ten thousand strokes per night. These summer thunderstorms erupt when moist air flows in from the Gulf of California and is forced upward by nearby mountains. The rising moisture condenses into thunderhead clouds that tower into a mushroom shape reaching sixty thousand feet above the ground.

Because of Tucson's high clouds, lightning here is the most dramatic to be found anywhere in North America. This is a five-minute time-exposure photograph of such a storm. The view is from a hill overlooking Tucson.

This photo of a storm over Florida's Lake Okeechobee spells double trouble: lightning and a twisting tornado called a *waterspout*. Florida is the lightning capital of the United States. The high humidity and heat produce almost daily summer thunderstorms and three times the number of lightning strokes of any other place in the country. In fact, ten percent of the people struck by lightning in the United States live in Florida. But lightning strikes in every state, sometimes very frequently. In March 1991, more than fifteen thousand lightning strikes resulted from a single six-hour storm stretching over Iowa, Illinois, Wisconsin, and Missouri. During that storm, the skies blazed with almost constant lightning.

Lightning can be made in a laboratory by an instrument called a *Van de Graaff static electricity generator.* It can generate millions of volts of artificial lightning from a metal sphere mounted at the top of an insulating column. In this demonstration at the Boston Museum of Science, the man in the metal "birdcage" is protected from the flashes of lightning made by a generator. The electricity passes through the metal frame and goes into the ground without harming the person inside. Grounded metal wires surrounding the exhibit protect visitors in the same way. Hardtop cars can shield motorists during a thunderstorm for the same reason, and grounded lightning rods can protect buildings.

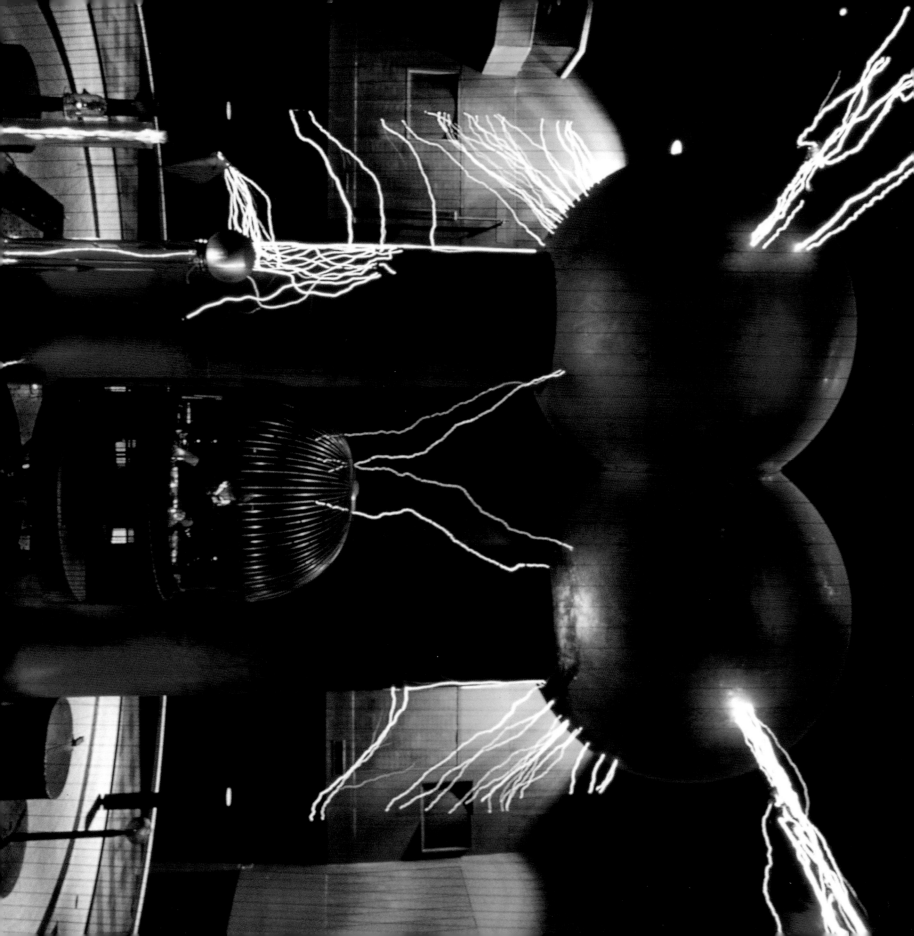

Lightning kills about one hundred people a year in the United States. Yet two hundred fifty more are hit by lightning each year and still survive. If you are caught out in the open in a lightning storm, stay away from places that are more likely to be hit: high ridges, open meadows, telephone poles, wire fences, rails, wet beaches, and single tall trees. A hardtop car is safe; bikes and open vehicles are not. The best thing to do if you feel tingly or your hair begins to stand on end is to crouch down with your hands off the ground and become "a basketball with legs." Don't lie down, because the ground can carry a charge.

If you are in water, get out as soon as possible. That's why workers at a water park near Tucson have to keep watching for the approach of distant storms. They also use lightning detectors that can register unseen flashes in the clouds above.

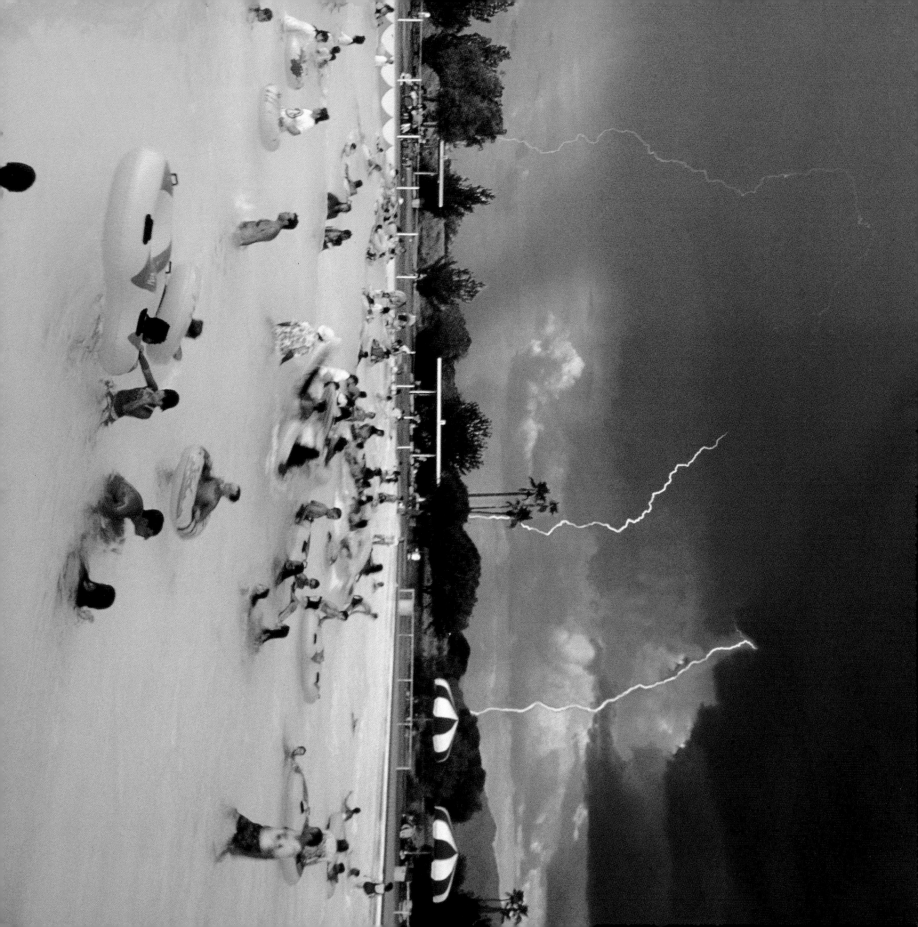

Scientists say that the recent discoveries of elves, sprites, and jets make it likely that there are more forms of lightning that we don't know anything about yet. Lightning flashes may even have been detected on other planets, such as Jupiter and Venus. Despite all we have learned since Ben Franklin's experiment over two hundred years ago, lightning remains a mystery that we are only slowly beginning to understand.